1 MONTH OF
FREE
READING

at
www.ForgottenBooks.com

By purchasing this book you are eligible for one month membership to ForgottenBooks.com, giving you unlimited access to our entire collection of over 1,000,000 titles via our web site and mobile apps.

To claim your free month visit:
www.forgottenbooks.com/free1122181

ISBN 978-0-331-42542-0
PIBN 11122181

WASHINGTON 25, D. C.

Official Business

FOR RELEASE MONDAY, FEBRUARY 27, 1956

VOLUME 72

NUMBER 9

CONTENTS

PAGE

(Continued on following page)

UNITED STATES DEPARTMENT OF AGRICULTURE
FOREIGN AGRICULTURAL SERVICE
WASHINGTON 25, D.C.

CONTENTS

(Continued from cover page)

- - - - - - -

PUBLICATIONS RELATING TO U. S. FOREIGN AGRICULTURAL TRADE

Issued recently and available free upon request
(single copies) to persons in the U.S. from the
Foreign Agricultural Service, U.S. Department of
Agriculture, Washington 25, D. C.,   Room 5922.
Phone: REpublic 7-4142, Ext. 2445.

Foreign Agriculture magazine, February issue.

Second Survey Confirms Record World Corn Crop. Foreign Agriculture
Circular FG 3-56.

Brazil Nut Situation. Foreign Agriculture Circular FN 1-56.

RENEWED GREEK-ITALIAN TRADE
AGREEMENT INCLUDES TOBACCO

The Greek-Italian Trade Agreement was extended December 22, 1955 for one year following the conclusion of negotiations in Athens between representatives of the two countries.

The agreement was made retroactive to July 1, 1955, and is to remain in force until June 30, 1956. It includes Greek tobacco as one of the items to be exported in exchange for Italian goods. Italian imports of Greek leaf tobacco during the July-June periods of 1953-54 and 1954-55 totaled about 4.1 and 5.5 million pounds, respectively.

AUSTRIAN TOBACCO IMPORTS
UP 33.5 PERCENT

Imports of unmanufactured tobacco by the Austrian Tobacco Monopoly during the first 9 months of 1955 totaled 15.1 million pounds -- up 33.5 percent from the 11.3 million pounds imported during the corresponding period of 1954.

Most of the increase occurred in larger takings of United States, Turkish and Brazilian leaf. Also, there were slight increases in imports from other sources except Yugoslavia. New sources of leaf during January-September 1955 were obtained from Hungary and the Central African Federation.

Austria: Imports of unmanufactured tobacco during the
           January-September periods, 1954-55

Country of Origin	January-September 1954	January-September 1955
	1,000 pounds	1,000 pounds
United States...................:	3,904	5,562
Brazil..........................:	147	638
Turkey..........................:	1,564	3,297
Yugoslavia......................:	992	-
Greece..........................:	2,881	2,920
Hungary.........................:	-	176
Bulgaria........................:	1,102	1,415
India...........................:	638	770
Italy...........................:	14	18
Central Africa Federation.......:	-	124
Indonesia.......................:	59	117
Other...........................:	2	52
Total...................:	11,303	15,089

Source: Statistik des Aussenhandels Osterreichs, Erstes bis drittes
         Vierteljahr 1955

TOBACCO INCLUDED IN RENEWED
FINNISH-ITALIAN TRADE AGREEMENT

  The Finnish-Italian Trade Agreement was extended for one year following the conclusion of negotiations held in Rome on October 10, 1955 between
representatives of the two countries. It was made retroactive to October
1, 1955, and is to remain in force until September 30, 1956. The new
agreement, which supplements the original agreement of May 5, 1951, includes
220,000 pounds of Italian tobacco as one of the items to be exported in
exchange for Finnish consumer and industrial goods. Finnish imports of
Italian leaf during 1953 and 1954 totaled about 68,000 and 37,000 pounds,
respectively.

LARGER RHODESIAN FLUE-CURED
CROP EXPECTED IN 1956

  Preliminary reports indicate that flue-cured tobacco production in
the Central African Federation will be about 144 million pounds in 1956 or
13 million pounds more than in 1955. However, production of dark tobaccos,
especially fire-cured, in 1956 is expected to decline to about 13.7 million
pounds or 9 percent below the 1955 level.

FEDERATION of the RHODESIAS AND NYASALAND: Estimated production of
tobacco in 1956, acreage and production

Type	1955		1956	
	Acres	1,000 pounds	Acres	1,000 pounds
Flue-cured............:	182,500	130,854	193,000	144,200
Fire-cured............:	30,460	15,023	28,250	13,700
Turkish...............:	450	185	550	220
Burley................:	3,000	220	1,000	500
Dark air-cured........:	4,500	2,321	4,200	2,100

  Rhodesian farmers are speeding up curing of flue-cured tobacco by
injecting steam into barns to raise temperatures quickly to 100° Fahrenheit
for coloring the leaf. This rapid temperature rise also reduces the development of barn spot. Faster curing is of extreme importance in Rhodesia as the
shortage of curing barns is a major factor limiting flue-cured production.

  Farmers there are also feeling the effects of rising operating costs.
The major operating expenses reported to be increasing in recent years are
wages, fertilizer, fuel and maintenace costs.

PAKISTAN EXPECTS LARGER
TOBACCO CROP IN 1956

Tobacco production in Pakistan is expected to increase from 200 million pounds harvested in 1955 from 197 thousand acres to 211 million pounds in 1956 from 207 thousand acres. Production of flue-cured tobacco is expected to increase from 8 million pounds in 1955 to 10 million pounds in 1956, a rise of about 25 percent.

Flue-cured tobacco production in the Northwest Frontier Province is threatened by a disease which damages the roots with an effect similar to root rot. At present, only flue-cured varieties are being attacked; Nicotiana Rustica or Desi types appear to be immune.

Production of cigarettes continues to increase with an output of 5.3 billion in 1955 compared with 4.5 billion in 1954 with further expansion expected in 1956 as shortages occurred periodically during the past year. New machinery and plant capacity for increasing cigarette output will be brought into production this year.

INCREASED INDIAN TOBACCO
CROP EXPECTED IN 1956

An increase of about 5 percent is expected in India's 1956 tobacco crop. This would amount to about 582 million pounds from 900 thousand acres compared with 555 million pounds produced in 1955 from 860 thousand acres. Production of Virginia tobacco is expected to increase to 125 million pounds in 1956 compared with 119 million in 1955.

EMBARGO ON CERTAIN YUGOSLAV AGRICULTURAL EXPORTS CONTINUES

According to the Yugoslav press, early in January the Economic Committee of the Federal Economic Council issued two decisions affecting the foreign trade of the country. Both decisions were made effective as of January 1 and were made to help stabilize the prices and supplies of the domestic market.

The first decision, which bans the export of various industrial and agricultural products, replaces a similar one of January 1, 1955, and includes the following agricultural and food products, most of which were included in the decision of 1955: wheat, barley, rye, oats, buckwheat, millet, all kinds of flour, soybeans, rapeseed, sunflower seed, cottonseed, hemp, clover, alfalfa, heifers, fats and edible oils, tallow, cheese, bacon, sugar, blood and fish meal, concentrated fodder, sugar beet cuttings, oil meal, bran, molasses and powdered milk. In case export permits had been issued during 1955 for certain of these products, the Foreign Trade Administration may renew the permit.

The following products may be exported only with a permit issued by the Foreign Trade Administration and export will be also restricted to seasons when domestic consumption is not highest: cattle, fattened hogs, horses, sheep, goats, beef, pork, horsemeat, mutton, feathers, and beans.

The second decision pertains to the system of import and export co-efficients which actually is a system of multiple rates of exchange meant to regulate imports and exports. The value of the coefficient which varies with each commodity, is applied to the rate of exchange to determine the dinar equivalents for the exporter or importer as a means of stimulating or limiting trade in either direction. Theoretically, exports can be discouraged and a better domestic supply insured by a low export coefficient on certain commodities, while at the same time a low import coefficient will encourage the import of commodities in short supply.

The decision includes reductions in the values of export coefficients for agricultural and food products, thus reducing the dinar proceeds of exports. This is in line with the change in structure of Yugoslav exports away from agricultural products which has been taking place since the war.

EGYPTIAN ONION EXPORTS
EXPECTED TO INCREASE

Exports of onions from Port Said are expected to reach 2,000,000 bags this season, according to the Port Said Chamber of Commerce. This compares with 1,200,000 bags shipped last year.

The Onion Market in Port Said will be opened on February 29.

U. S. RICE EXPORTS
ABOVE A YEAR AGO

Rice exports from the United States in December amounted to 707,000 bags (100 pounds) in terms of milled rice as compared with 446,000 in the corresponding month of 1954. Shipments, however, were the smallest in 4 months. Principal exports were to Ouba and India, but those to Japan declined.

Exports in terms of milled rice during the August-December period of the current marketing year totaled 5,361,000 bags, a gain of 1,434,000 bags, or 37 percent, above the like period of a year earlier. Quantities increased to Japan, Liberia, and West Germany, and rice was shipped to countries that did not import rice from the United States last year, such as Indochina, India, French West Africa, the Philippine Republic, and Bolivia.

RICE: United States exports to specified countries, by
classification, December 1955 1/

Country of destination	Rough				
	Unmilled	In of			
	Bags	Bags	Bags	Bags	
estern Hemisphere:					
Canada.............................:	5,427	3,527	5,732	13,047:	22
Mexico.............................:	0	0	0	10:	
British Honduras...................:	0	0	1,000	2,000:	3
Costa Rica.........................:	500	325	0	5,218:	5
Canal Zone.........................:	0	0	0	32:	
Bermuda............................:	0	0	0	477:	
Bahamas............................:	0	0	0	40:	
Cuba...............................:	12,601	8,191	22,390	282,176:	312
Jamaica............................:	0	0	1,344	104:	1
Haiti..............................:	0	0	0	850:	
Dominican Republic.................:	0	0	0	100:	
French West Indies.................:	0	0	100	0:	
Netherlands Antilles...............:	0	0	0	4,529:	4
Colombia...........................:	15,400	10,010	0	0:	10
Venezuela..........................:	1,000	650	0	19:	
Total...........................:					
urope:					
Belgium and Luxembourg.............:	0	0	26,614	560:	27
Denmark............................:	0	0	0	250:	
Greece.............................:	0	0	0	167:	
Netherlands........................:	0	0	1,097	0:	1
Sweden.............................:	0	0	0	495:	
Switzerland........................:	0	0	0	5,288:	5
Total...........................:				6 6	4
sia:					
India..............................:	0	0	0	204,706:	204
Israel.............................:	0	0	0	4,501:	4
Japan..............................:	0	0	0	58,190:	58
Philippines........................:	0	0	5,511	0:	5
Nonsei and Nonpo Islands, n.e.s...:	0	0	0	200:	
Saudi Arabia.......................:	0	0	0	12,800:	12
Total...........................:					
rust territory of the Pacific......:					
iberia.............................:					
ther...............................:					
Total world.................:					

/ Preliminary.   2/ Starting with January 1954, "other" includes shipments value
ess than $500 each when the number of such shipments to a country is few.

ource: Bureau of the Census.

RICE: United States exports, in terms of milled, to specified
        countries, December 1955, with comparisons 1/

	1,000 bags	1,000 bags	1,000 bags	1,000 bags	1,000 bags	
Western Hemisphere:						
Canada	633	560	272	260	42	
British Honduras	17	33	17	13	3	
Honduras	3	30	14	15	4	
Haiti	2	124	54	2	2/	
Cuba	4,755	3,391	2,426	1,608	282	
Netherlands Antilles	53	38	17	15	3	
Bolivia	5	0	0	110	0	
Colombia	314	205	173	10	14	
Venezuela	215	84	32	1	27	
Other countries	30	10	2	19	0	
Total						
Europe:						
Belgium and Luxembourg	206	460	155	151	24	
Greece	11	5	5	2/	5	
Ireland	0	16	16	0	0	
West Germany	29	38	9	27	0	
Netherlands	12	71	7	5	6	
Sweden	1	72	68	7	2	
Switzerland	57	53	47	16	3	
Other countries	24 :3	99	5	3	0	
Total						
Asia:						
India	0	0	0	205	0	
Indochina	0	0	0	220	0	
Korea, Republic of 4/	590	2/	0	0	0	
Japan	8,538	4,125	392	2,279	2	
Saudi Arabia	130	136	111	47	23	
Philippines	2/	25	0	17 ::	0	
Other countries	25	11	6	6	1	
Total						
Total Oceania	17	19				
Liberia	67	219				
French West Africa	0	0				
Other Africa	6	10				
Other :6	8 :6	14 :6				
Total world						

1/ Includes brown, broken, screenings and brewers' rice, and rough rice conve
terms of milled at 65 percent. 2/ Less than 500 bags. 3/ Includes 58,000 ba
Trieste and 23,000 bags to Austria. 4/ Adjusted to include all programs of t
Department of Defense and the International Cooperation Administration. 6/ S
with January 1954, "other" includes shipments valued at less than $500 each w
number of such shipments to a country in a given month is few.

Source: Bureau of the Census, except as noted.

NEW CANNING FACTORY ESTABLISHED
IN SOUTH AFRICA

A new canning factory, the Tulbach Fruit Industry (PTY) Ltd., has recently been established near Cape Town, Union of South Africa. The factory was built in a record time of 5 months, at a cost of $700,000, subscribed by its 50 stockholders.

Currently employing some 800 non-skilled workers and about 12 technical and supervisory workers, the factory uses mostly equipment and materials of South African origin, although a few machines have been imported from America.

The Tulbach factory cans, in season, apricots, peaches, plums, and pears. In May and June, the "off-season", string beans and guavas are canned. Also small quantities of apricot and peach jam are canned. Most of the fruit used by the factory is grown within a 5-mile radius of the factory.

During the first year of operation, (November 1954-October 1955) approximately 4,000,000 pounds of fruit and jams were processed. Of this amount about 2,500,000 pounds were exported to Europe, mostly to the United Kingdom. This year's output is expected to more than double last year's. The "Capehill" products have been commended for their quality and are said to be gaining in popularity on both the export and domestic markets.

C O R R E C T I O N -- (Cotton exports under P.L. 480)

In the tables in Foreign Crops and Markets, of February 20, 1956, Page 227, listing United States cotton exports under Title I of Public Law 480, the unit at the top of the first column should have been "dollars" (not bales.)

VENEZUELA SEEN AS SOURCE OF FRESH MILK FOR
NETHERLANDS WEST INDIES

The milk of Venezuela's Caracas milk shed is being considered as a source of supply for the Dutch West Indies. A businessman from Willemstad, Curacao, recently arrived in Caracas to investigate the possibility of expressing pasteurized fluid milk·from the Venezuelan surplus to Curacao and Aruba, N.W.I. He described the presently available milk as high priced and of poor quality, due to the time lapse between pasteurization and arrival in the Indies. He expressed belief that milk can be flown from Venezuela to the Indies at less cost and in less time than the milk now coming from the United States and the Netherlands.

The flight from Maiquetia, a coastal city near Caracas, to Curacao, takes 40 minutes. A flight from Puerto Cabello, another Venezuelan coastal city nearer the milk producing area, would require less time.

The population of the islands that make up the Netherlands West Indies-Curacao, Aruba, and Bonaire, is about 150,000.

The Netherlands West Indies has decreased its takings of American fresh milk over recent years. During the early 1950's, this market imported about 425 thousand pounds from the United States annually. The preliminary 1955 figure shows about 125 thousand pounds.

FINNISH MILK AND BUTTER
PRODUCTION INCREASES

Due to an early winter upsurge, Finnish milk production during 1955 may not be as low as early forecasts indicated, (see Foreign Crops and Markets, January 23, 1956). The October-November 1955 production sold to fluid milk distributors and butter and cheese manufacturers, is estimated at 7 percent over the 503 million pounds marketed during the same months in 1954.

The increase was attributed to a better quality 1955 hay, increased availability of, and lower subsidized prices for, imported feed concentrates, and an increase in the producer price of milk. However, extended milk collection routes, resulting in decreased churning of farm butter, and the farmer's need for additional income due to reduced timber sales have also contributed to the rise in distribution receipts.

Factory butter production during the October-November 1955 period is also estimated at 7 percent above the same period in 1954, and stood at 15.3 million pounds. This increased production promised a better supply situation throughout the winter than was formerly forecast. (see Foreign Crops and Markets, February 6, 1956.)

Butter stocks on January 21 stood at slightly over 4.7 million pounds and are believed substantial enough to supplement the gradually increasing production so that further importations during the winter and spring will be unnecessary.

NEW MILK PLANT IN COLOMBIA

The city of Bucaramanga, Colombia, just north of Bogota, has a new milk plant which is a cooperative and has a capacity of 75,000 to 80,000 quarts a day. The operation is modeled after that of a successful cooperative in Barranquilla. The equipment is entirely of British manufacture but does not include a homogenization unit.

NEW MILK PLANTS IN INDIA UNDER CONSIDERATION

The Government of the state of Andhra, India is considering the erection of two dairy plants for the processing of milk products. Andhra is in the southeastern part of India, just above Madras City, and has a population of over 20 million. One of the plants would be at Ongole and the other would be in the delta area.

A proposal has also been made to set up a milk control board to control the supply and quality of milk. The control board would also coordinate milk supply schemes undertaken both by private and public agencies.

SWISS DAIRY SITUATION

Milk deliveries to dairy plants in Switzerland during the first 11 months of 1955 were about 1 percent below comparable 1954. Several factors contributed to this reduction in milk for commercial purposes. Among these were the decline in the number of cows as a result of the tightening of the anti-tubercle bacillus campaign, the fact that the quality of the hay which was not uniformly good in all areas of Switzerland, and a greater utilization of milk on farms.

In this period, cheese production was up 3.8 percent, condensed and dried milk 5.1 percent. On the other hand, butter production dropped 10 percent, but this shortage in supplies was covered by imports.

U. S. WHEAT AND FLOUR EXPORTS SLIGHTLY
BELOW THAT OF A YEAR AGO

United States wheat and flour exports during the first 6 months (July-December) of the 1955-56 fiscal year amounted to 121 million bushels compared with 122 million during the first 6 months of the 1954-55 fiscal year. Shipments in the form of wheat declined from 102 million bushels to 97 million. Those in the form of flour, however, increased from a grain equivalent of 20 million bushels to 24 million.

A large reduction took place in exports of wheat as grain to the United Kingdom, West Germany, Brazil, Spain, Belgium-Luxembourg, Norway and Yogoslavia. On the other hand, much larger shipments were made to Japan, the Netherlands, Italy, Peru, Chile and Colombia. With respect to flour, practically every country took just a little more than during the same period a year ago, except the British West Indies, Colombia, Bolivia, Chile, Norway, the Netherlands and West Germany.

United States Wheat and Flour Exports During Stated Periods

	(Thousands of bushels, grain equivalent)					
Western Hemisphere						
Canada	2	45	47	1,296	163	1,45
Mexico	8	5	13	515	8	5.
Central America	263	1,687	1,950	383	2,211	2,5
Cuba	681	1,709	2,390	523	1,710	2,2
British West Indies	-	1,337	1,337	-	1,217	1,2
Columbia	94	128	222	1,116	42	1,1
Venezuela	66	1,441	1,507	46	2,430	2,4
Peru	711	66	777	2,776	96	2,8
Bolivia	1,189	576	1,765	388	291	6
Chile	-	54	54	1,388	4	1,3
Brazil	7,956	2/	7,956	3,003	181	3,18
Others	144	1,781	1,925	253	1,928	2,18
Total	11,114	8,829	19,943	11,687	10,281	21,9
Europe						
Norway	1,756	805	2,561	360	684	1,0
United Kingdom	15,496	188	15,684	4,848	673	5,5
Netherlands	3,950	2,162	6,112	9,708	2,045	11,7
Belgium-Luxembourg	3,288	10	3,298	1,738	13	1,7
West Germany	14,571	63	14,634	9,371	1	9,3
Spain	2,254	-	2,254	545	-	5
Portugal	1,309	136	1,445	978	176	1,1
Italy	388	12	400	2,925	590	3,5
Yugoslavia	15,945	4	15,949	14,738	6	14,7
Greece	3,661	2	3,663	4,013	4	4,0
Others	1,504	63	1,567	234	31	2
Total	64,122	3,445	67,567	49,458	4,223	53,
Asia						
Lebanon	3	591	594	-	1,118	1,1
Israel	2,752	6	2,758	2,906	5	2,9
Indonesia	-	83	83	-	356	3
Japan	14,559	329	14,888	24,472	572	25,0
Philippines	1	2,044	2,045	-	2,042	2,0
Others	8,086	2,288	10,374	5,553	2,464	8,0
Total	25,401	5,341	30,742	32,931	6,557	3
Others						
Africa	1,388	2,701	4,089	2,808	2,838	
Oceania	-	7	7	-	9	
Unspecified	-	-	-	4	111	
Total	1,388	2,				
World Total	102,025	20,323	122,348	96,888	24,019	

1/ Wholly of U.S. wheat.
2/ Less than 500 bushels.

WHEAT FLOUR PRODUCTION IN FRENCH
WEST AFRICA

There are two flour mills in French West Africa, with a combined
annual capacity of 90,000 metric tons of flour. Both mills are located
in Dakar, which is the capital and chief port of French West Africa,
and in the Senegal Territory. The combined production of these two mills
exceeds the total requirements for all French West Africa which has a
population of more than 17 million.

The Moulins de L'A.O.F., (L'Afrique Occidentale Francaise), a
privately owned and managed mill, is now operating 24 hours a day, 6
days a week. Its total annual production of 15,000 metric tons of flour
is sold within the Senegal Territory, which has a population of approximately 2 million, and where consumption of flour is 30,000 metric tons
annually. The wheat comes from Morocco and France. A very good quality
flour is being produced and there seems to be in good demand for it. The
company is planning to build another mill of greater capacity at Abidjan
in the Ivory Coast.

The other mill in French West Africa, Grandes Moulins de Dakar,
seems to be very closely tied in with the Central Government. Its
capacity is 75,000 metric tons of flour, but since there is now a
surplus of flour, and the other mill is firmly established with the
public, this mill is operating at only half of capacity. It imports
60,000 tons of wheat annually, with 90 percent coming from Morocco and
10 percent from France.

The inflated price system within the French Union prevents competi-
tion with world prices but if France should decide to permit the purchase
of wheat in the international market there would be a definite danger to
the United States flour market in British West Africa. In 1954-55,
British West Africa imported approximately 100,000 metric tons of wheat
and wheat flour, with two-thirds of such imports coming from the United
States and the other one-third from Canada. However, labor costs in
French West Africa have greatly increased so that production costs might
remain above those of the United States and Canada even if the wheat came
from outside the French Union.

The position of wheat flour markets in West Africa should be followed
closely.

DECEMBER 1955 EXPORTS GRASS AND LEGUME
SEEDS INCREASED OVER PREVIOUS MONTH

December 1955 exports of grass and legume seeds increased more than
900 thousand pounds over the preceding month but continued to reflect the
sharp decline from record levels reached last year. The only exceptions
are Redtop and Timothy which show marked increases over previous years.

U.S. EXPORTS: Grass and Legume Seeds, December 1955,
with comparisons

Kind of Seed	December		July 1, 1954, to Dec. 31, 1954	July 1, 1955, to Dec. 31, 1955
	1954	1955		
	1,000 pounds	1,000 pounds	1,000 pounds	1,000 pounds
Alfalfa............:	2,138	1,056	7,176	3,529
Alsike............:	130	0	424	58
Other clovers.........:	3,459	282	7,578	1,037
Fescue............:	181	108	918	420
Ky. bluegrass.........:	233	50	645	217
Orchard............:	27	0	158	36
Redtop............:	50	177	135	387
Timothy............:	91	202	254	555
Other grasses.........:	2,546	787	15,340	2,606
Total.............:	8,855	2,662	32,628	8,845

Compiled from official statistics of the Bureau of the Census.

COTTON CONSUMPTION IN CANADA
CONTINUES AT DECEMBER LEVEL

Cotton mill consumption in Canada amounted to 32,500 bales (500 pounds gross) in January 1956, to continue the approximate level of December 1955 consumption of 32,900 bales, but well above January a year ago, when 28,000 bales were consumed.

Mill consumption for the 6-month period, August-January 1955-56 amounted to 200,000 bales, increasing 16 percent over consumption of 173,000 bales in the corresponding period of 1954-55.

U.S. COTTON EXPORTS
CONTINUE TO LAG

Exports of cotton from the United States in December 1955 amounted to 166,000 bales of 500 pounds gross (159,000 running bales) making an August-December total of 698,000 bales (665,000 running bales). This total is only 41 percent of the 1,692,000 bales exported during the corresponding period of last year. The slump in exports began in June 1955, and represents the lowest level since 1944-45.

Most of the decline from last year has been in exports to Western European countries and Canada, with reductions amounting to 77 and 74 percent, respectively. Exports to Japan, Korea, and Taiwan (Formosa) have dropped only slightly from the earlier period.

UNITED STATES: Exports of cotton by countries of destination, averages
1935-39 and 1945-49; annual 1953 and 1954; August-December 1954-55
and 1955-56

(Equivalent bales of 500 pounds gross)

Country of destination	Year beginning August 1				August-December	
	Averages 1935-39	1945-49	1953	1954	1954-55	1955-56
	1,000 bales	1,000 bales	1,000 bales	1,000 bales	1,000 bales	1,000 bales
Austria................:	0:1/	36:	42:	15:	8:	6
Belgium...............:	169:	131:	68:	66:	42:	2
Czechoslovakia........:	65:	57:	0:	0:	0:	0
Denmark...............:	33:	14:	23:	21:	9:	0
Finland...............:	35:	21:	10:	13:	0:	15
France................:	662:	575:	475:	416:	268:	53
Germany, West.........:	511:	340:	389:	350:	188:	28
Italy.................:	442:	489:	269:	249:	142:	24
Netherlands...........:	107:	131:	104:	95:	44:	1
Norway................:	17:	7:	14:	12:	6:	0
Poland and Danzig.....:	180:	69:	0:	0:	0:	0
Portugal..............:	36:	2/ :	0:	11:	0:	0
Spain.................:	108:	69:	167:	197:	34:	67
Sweden................:	115:	12:	43:	51:	30:	2
Switzerland...........:	11:	26:	24:	37:	29:	8
United Kingdom........:	1,346:	488:	422:	421:	228:	37
Yugoslavia............:	17:	47:	40:	103:	30:	1
Other Europe..........:	31:3/	33:	10:	9:	2:	1
Total Europe.........:	3,885:	2,545:	2,100:	2,066:	1,060:	245
Canada................:	301:	275:	237:	307:	137:	36
Chile.................:	9:	20:	27:	10:	7:	4
Colombia..............:	20:	24:	7:	2:	1:	9
Cuba..................:	11:	16:	20:	19:	13:	1
India.................:	52:	86:	161:	61:	48:	1
China.................:	117:	401:	0:	0:	0:	0
French Indochina......:	22:	6:	16:	0:	0:	0
Indonesia.............:	2/:	5:	22:	27:	12:	6
Japan.................:	1,142:	585:	1,005:	678:	260:	254
Korea, Republic of....:	4/:5/	48:	96:	170:	68:	47
Taiwan (Formosa).......:	4/:	1:	110:	120:	35:	50
Australia.............:	9:	7:	45:	52:	23:	9
Other countries.......:	21:	46:6/	68:7/	73:	28:	36
Total 500-lb. Bales..:	5,589:	4,065:	3,914:	3,585:	1,692:	698
Total Running Bales..:	5,300:	3,917:	3,761:	3,447:	1,626:	665

1/ 4-year average. 2/ Less than 500 bales. 3/ Includes Greece 21. 4/
If any, included in "Other countries." 5/ 3-year average. 6/ Israel 12,
Ethiopia 11. 7/ Israel 20, French Morocco 11.

Compiled from official records of the Bureau of the Census.

WEST GERMANY IMPORTS LESS
UNITED STATES COTTON

West Germany's imports of United States cotton dropped sharply in
the August-October 1955 quarter, amounting to 26,000 bales (500 pounds
gross) or only 9 percent of total imports, as compared with 79,000 bales
and 28 percent of the total for August-October 1954. Total imports during the current period amounted to 280,000 bales, or practically the
same as the 278,000 bales imported a year earlier.

Imports from Mexico and Nicaragua supplanted those from the United
States in the period under review, and increased amounts were also registered from Peru, the Sudan, Turkey, and the U.S.S.R. Declines were
shown in imports from Brazil and Egypt. Quantities imported in August-
October 1955, with figures for the corresponding period of 1954 in paren-
theses were: Mexico 71,000 bales (43,000); Nicaragua 33,000 (17,000);
the United States 26,000 (79,000); Peru 23,000 (11,000); Egypt 20,000
(22,000) the Sudan 19,000 (4,000); Brazil 19,000 (56,000); Turkey 14,000
(12,000); and the U.S.S.R. 13,000 (none).

West German cotton mills worked almost at full capacity during the
quarter. Production of yarns was 2.5 percent above the already high production for the same quarter of the previous year. The percentage of
cellulose staple fiber used in these yarns was also higher, however, and
consumption of raw cotton was therefore slightly less than that used a
year ago, 314,000 bales as compared with 319,000 in the earlier period.
Cotton mill stocks declined during the quarter from the 220,000 bales
held on August 1, 1955, to an estimated 186,000 bales on October 31,
1955.

COTTON CONSUMPTION IN THE
PHILIPPINE REPUBLIC

Increasing interest in the development of the cotton spinning industry in the Philippine Republic has been evident in the last several
years. At present there are about 47,000 spindles in operation, and
cotton consumption averages about 8,000 bales (500 pounds gross) per
year. There is a small cottage industry which uses most of the locally-
grown cotton in the production of household articles. Cotton imports by
the Philippine Republic are almost entirely from the United States, and
average about 8,000 bales annually.

Philippine cotton production in recent years has averaged between
300 and 400 bales per year from an area varying from 1,000 to 3,000 acres.
Historically, some cotton has been produced in the Republic for many
years. Plans for increasing cotton acreage to a possible 15,000 or
20,000 acres have been reported, although the numerous problems, which
have limited production in the past, still exist. These are mainly un-
seasonal rains, difficulties in insect control, plant diseases, and
needed improvement of cultivation practices.

URUGUAY TO BUY ARGENTINE CATTLE

An Uruguayan decree issued February 1, 1956, approved in principle the purchase of 60,000 head of canner cattle from Argentina.

Some sources have indicated that authority will be granted to import an additional 140,000 head of Argentine slaughter cattle and some breeding stock in 1956.

DANISH-WEST GERMAN
TRADE AGREEMENT

Exports of slaughter cattle from Denmark to Western Germany this year will be limited to 225,000 to 250,000 head on the basis of a recent trade agreement between the two countries. Under the agreement, Danish exports of hogs and hog carcasses will be limited to 20,000 to 25,000 metric tons, lard to 8,000 metric tons and variety meats to 21,000 D.M. ($5,040). These quantities are essentially the same as those for the previous year. Germany's exports to Denmark will be mostly industrial goods.

During 1955 there was a substantial increase in exports of slaughter cattle from Denmark to Western Germany but exports of hogs were smaller than a year earlier.

U. S. SHARE OF FOREIGN COTTON
MARKETS DECREASES SHARPLY

The United States share of foreign cotton markets in 12 of the major cotton importing countries declined sharply in the early months of the 1955-56 cotton marketing year, and imports by all but one of these countries registered major declines.

Imports of United States cotton by Canada dropped from 96 to 39 percent of all cotton imports; those of France from 32 to 13 percent; Western Germany from 30 to 9 percent; and the United Kingdom from 36 to 16 percent. Other declines occurred in Belgium's imports of United States cotton which dropped from 12 to 7 percent; the Netherlands from 25 to 5 percent; Switzerland from 34 to 10 percent; Hong Kong from 5 to 1 percent; and Japan from 39 to 17 percent. Only Spain showed increased imports of United States cotton, which expanded from 24 to 78 percent of the total.

(See table on following page 258)

PERU FACED WITH
TEMPORARY BEEF SURPLUS

The drought in Peru has increased cattle slaughter and the arrival of 1,200 tons of Argentinian beef, and 8,800 head of cattle from Central America has created difficulties for the meat packing industry. (See Foreign Crops and Markets, February 6, 1956, page 164). These imports had been contracted for prior to the onset of the drought. The current beef surplus, which is regarded to be only temporary, has not as yet resulted in lower retail beef prices.

A group of United States, Peruvian, and British investors are carrying out a large scale program for the development of Peru's meat packing industry. They have set up a company which will furnish equipment and supplies to cattle producers, construct an abattoir at Juliaca and ship beef from the abattoir in refrigerated cars to Mataroni, (where cold storage facilities of 300 metric ton capacity will be built). The beef will then be sent by refrigerated ships to Lima.

The plant at Juliaca is expected to begin operations in about a year. These operations should do a great deal toward long run improvement in Peru's situation. It is generally agreed, however, that a serious beef shortage is in the offing in Peru, primarily due to the heavy slaughter of drought-stricken cattle at this time.

LARGE EXPORTS OF U. S. MEAT
PRODUCTS TO THE NETHERLANDS

During 1955 United States exports of packing house products to the Netherlands continued large, while United States imports of hams dropped substantially, according to Netherlands' trade statistics. The Netherlands is the largest importer of United States packing house products in Continental Europe. During 1955, it was the largest United States export market for inedible tallows and greases and variety meats (offals), the second largest for cattle hides, third for pork, fourth for calf and kip skins and seventh for lard.

Imports of United States packing house products by the Netherlands during the first 11 months of 1955 were valued at $22.8 million. Imports of these products from the United States during the whole year 1954 amounted to $27.3 million. In addition to the imports stated above Dutch transit dealers found outlets for substantial additional quantities of frozen and canned meats, lard, tallows and greases, sausage casings and hides from the United States for sale in third countries. The transit trade of United States products during the first 11 months of 1955 included 69,400 metric tons of lard and other animal fats and greases, 1,200 tons of hides and 900 tons of frozen and canned meats (these figures are amounts warehoused under bond, small amounts were subsequently imported by the Netherlands and included as Netherlands' imports).

During the first 11 months of 1955 the dollars earned by the Netherlands through exports of canned hams to the United States were not quite sufficient to pay for the packing house products imported from the United States. Ham exports amounted to $22.4 million. In volume, exports of hams to the United States during the full year 1955 were about one-fifth less than a year earlier.

The United States supplied 55 percent of Netherlands import requirements of meat, 84 percent of the imported animal fats and 23 percent of the hides brought in from all sources during the first 11 months of 1955.

The Netherlands: Imports of packing house products from the United States, 1954 and January-November 1955 1/

Item	Imports from the United States		Percentage of Netherlands imports supplied by United States	
	1954	Jan-Nov. 1955	1954	Jan-Nov. 1955
	---Metric tons---			
Frozen beef................	9,408	8,950		
Frozen lamb and mutton.....	-	99		
Frozen pork................	573	1,343		
Salted meat................	430	-		
Total meat	10,411	10,392	53	55
Sausage casings............	220	234		
Offals for chemical and medicinal preparations...	394	347	67	60
Lard, tallows, and other animal fats..............	75,647	64,181	82	84
Hides......................	11,350	8,924	30	23

1/ Netherlands trade statistics; excludes transit trade.

U. S. LARD EXPORTS UP
100 MILLION POUNDS IN 1955

Lard exports from the United States in 1955 totaled 562 million pounds. This is an increase of nearly 100 million pounds from 1954 shipments and well over 3 times the prewar movement. The larger export of lard last year was due primarily to increased domestic production and lower prices.

United States: Exports of lard, including rendered pork fat,
by country of destination, average 1935-39, annual 1953-55

(1,000 pounds)

Continent & Country	Average 1935-39	1953	1954	1955 1/
North America:				
Canada	2,077	7,020	3,292	7,308
Costa Rica	1,186	7,513	7,028	8,177
Cuba	39,912	142,391	158,326	166,965
Dominican Republic	460	148	40	0
El Salvador	5	4,780	4,048	5,290
Guatemala	395	7,311	8,934	12,513
Haiti	645	7,098	5,874	5,780
Mexico	5,499	39,983	30,650	19,948
Netherlands Antilles	307	1,856	446	323
Canal Zone	157	1,290	682	1,018
Panama, Rep. of	1,033	6,809	9,432	3,086
Other	284	1,648	1,326	2,602
Total	51,960	227,847	230,078	233,010
South America:				
Brazil	1	10,381	4	6
Bolivia	15	2,178	4,994	6,829
Colombia	3,741	633	2,358	2,852
Ecuador	801	12,102	9,000	2,763
Peru	32	15,373	4,836	9,200
Venezuela	3,221	1,326	712	1,649
Other	13	126	112	74
Total	7,824	42,119	22,016	23,373
Europe:				
Austria	2/	20,687	18,478	21,378
Belgium and Luxembourg	2,460	168	70	233
Czechoslovakia	1,654	0	0	0
France	29	8	1,538	25
Germany (Western)3/2/	2,536	34,316	49,584	68,671
Greece	1	0	0	0
Italy	707	15	118	289
Netherlands	330	34,576	14,294	19,204
Poland	39	0	0	661
Switzerland	218	606	2,216	293
United Kingdom	95,733	24,197	97,106	167,496
Yugoslavia	4	20,757	26,786	20,682
Other	1,937	4/ 12,858	356	862
Total	105,648	148,188	210,546	299,806
Soviet Union	4	0	0	0
Asia	36	4,387	2,340	3,727
Africa	158	16	0	20
Oceania	6	34	0	8
Grand Total	165,636	422,591	5/465,396	5/562,071

1/ Preliminary. 2/ Austria included with Germany. 3/ Prior to
January 1952, reported as Germany. 4/ Includes 11,890,000 pounds to
Sweden. 5/ Includes a small quantity, the final destination of which
has not yet been designated.
Compiled from official records of the Department of Commerce.

Heavier exports to Europe, the major area market in 1955, largely accounted for the overall increase in total shipments. Exports to the United Kingdom were up sharply for the second successive year and totaled 167 million pounds. Quantities going to Western Germany, Austria and the Netherlands also were larger than in 1954.

Total exports to North American countries were up moderately from the year before. Larger exports to Cuba, Canada, and Guatemala offset smaller shipments to Mexico and Panama. Cuba was the most important single market for United States lard from 1952 through 1954 but was second to the United Kingdom last year.

United States exports of lard to South America were slightly larger than in 1954 with the largest quantities going to Peru and Bolivia. Exports to Ecuador were substantially below previous years.

AUSTRALIAN WOOL EXPORTS
BY CURRENCY AREAS

During the 6-month period ending December 31, 1955, Australian wool exports were valued at about $363 million. Exports to sterling currency areas during this period totaled $101 million, compared with $123 million for the corresponding months of 1954. Exports to dollar areas in July-December period of 1955 were valued at $33 million representing a decline of $2 million, while exports to other currency areas increased from $199 million to $229 million.

AUSTRALIA: Exports of wool by currency areas,
July 1-December 31, 1954 and 1955 1/

Currency area	1954		1955	
	Quantity greasy basis	Value in U.S. dollars	Quantity greasy basis	Value in U.S. dollars
	Million pounds	Million dollars	Million pounds	Million dollars
Sterling................:	179	123	180	101
Dollar................:	50	35	56	33
Other................:	286	199	388	229
Total.........:	515	357	624	363

1/ Includes greasy, scoured, carbonized, tops, noils and waste wool.

Source: Commonwealth Bureau of Census and Statistics, Canberra, Australia.

MEXICO BUYS
U. S. SHEEP

On January 21, the Federal Secretary of Agriculture of Mexico
announced the purchase of 43,500 head of high-quality Rambouillet sheep
in the United States and Canada. Included in the purchase are 40,000
ewes and 3,500 rams.

The main purpose of the purchase is to eliminate Mexico's imports
of wool which amount to $8 million per year. Among other objectives are
diversification of farming, more efficient utilization of available lands,
increased rural purchasing power, and a larger meat supply. The sheep
will be distributed throughout the central provinces of Mexico. (See
Foreign Crops and Markets, December 12, 1955, page 676).

The first 5,000 sheep were delivered to farmers in the Guadalupe
Victoria area of Durango. The state of Durango formerly was a leading
sheep-raising region but now has only an estimated 300,000 head. It is
considered an ideal place to begin sheep improvement work because of
ready markets and past experience in sheep-raising.

MEXICO DEFINES
USE OF PERMITS

Late information from Mexico defines the types of permits required
for imports of live animals, animal fats, canned meats, glands and organs.
Permits for importation of these products may be authorized by either the
Ministries of Economy or Agriculture or the Director of Animal Sanitation.

The Ministry of Agriculture of Mexico requires import permits for in
shipments of all live animals, except baby chicks. The Director of
Animal Sanitation now authorizes imports of animal fats meeting sanitary
requirements and are covered by permits from the Ministry of Economy. The
Director of Animal Sanitation authorizes imports of canned meat products
without special permit. Imports of livestock glands and organs are sub-
ject to special permits by the Ministry of Agriculture.

NOVEMBER SUEZ SOYBEAN
TRAFFIC UP FROM 1954

Northbound shipments of soybeans in November totaled about 881,840
bushels, considerably above the 183,720 bushels shipped in the same month
in 1954. This brought the January-November total to 17,784,000 bushels
as compared with 11,574,000 bushels shipped during the same period in
1954. Of the November (1955) total, 698,000 bushels were reportedly
destined for German ports and 147,000 bushels for Belgium.

Vegetable oil shipments through November totaled 1,173 million pounds. The traffic during the same period in 1954 was 668 million. November shipments were close to 60 million pounds as compared with 75 million in 1954.

U. S. SOYBEAN EXPORTS AT RECORD HIGH; OIL EXPORTS UP SHARPLY

United States exports of soybeans during 1955 established a new record of 67,289,000 bushels and were 56 percent larger than the year before. Soybean oil exports at 68,976 short tons, crude oil basis, were 78 percent larger than in 1954 but only 27 percent of the record 257,875 tons exported in 1951. Bean shipments as such represented 84 percent of the total bean and oil exports, which aggregated 79.9 million bushels, bean equivalent basis. This total was 58 percent larger than in 1954 and 3 percent above the previous record, reached in 1951.

The heavy exports of soybeans in 1955 reflected a strong world demand for fats and oils and relatively low prices for soybeans in the latter half of the year. Also, German restrictions on imports of oilseeds for dollars were removed in May. Japan continued to be the major market for United States soybeans, taking a record volume of 21,937,000 bushels or almost one-third of the total exports. Shipments to Europe at 31,313,000 bushels were double those of the previous year and accounted for almost one-half the total. The major European markets were Western Germany and the Netherlands. Canadian purchases were slightly larger than in 1954.

Exports of soybean oil in the first half of 1955 were materially smaller than a year earlier, but large shipments to Spain and Greece in the second half, reflecting purchases to supplement short domestic supplies of olive oil, raised the year's total to a level well above 1954. The exports to Spain were the first since 1951, when 72,641 tons were shipped, also as a supplement to short olive oil supplies. The 1955 exports to Spain accounted for 50 percent of the total to all countries, and those to Greece, for 18 percent. Purchases by Canada, up 66 percent from 1954, accounted for 17 percent of the 1955 total.

(Table on following page)

U. S. FLAXSEED, LINSEED OIL EXPORTS DOWN SHARPLY FROM RECORD HIGH OF 1954

United States exports of flaxseed and linseed oil in 1955 were down sharply from 1954, when the volume marketed abroad reached an all-time peak reflecting large sales at low prices from Commodity Credit Corporation stocks to exporters. CCC stocks were substantially reduced in 1954 and by the end of 1955 were small. International market prices for flaxseed rose in 1955 to the United States market level, and there were some commercial exports of flaxseed.

(Continued on Page 255)

(Continued from preceding pa

UNITED STATES: Soybean and soybean oil exports by country
of destination, average 1935-39, annual 1954-1955

Country of destination	Soybeans			Soybean oil 1/		
	Average 1937-39 2/	1954 3/ 4/	1955 3/	Average 1935-39	1954 3/ 4/	195
	1,000 bushels			Short tons		
North America:						
Canada.............	1,197:	7,497:	7,787:	76:	7,205:	11
Cuba...............	5/ :	5/ :	5/ :	1,917:	1,587:	3
Other..............	62:	— :	1:	467:	313:	2
Total..........						
South America.........						
Europe:	:	:	:	:	:	
Austria............	6/ :	— :	37:	— :	— :	
Belgium-Luxembourg..	15:	204:	1,324:	— :	451:	
Denmark............	606:	1,365:	3,947:	— :	— :	
Finland............	18:	163:	186:	65:	— :	
France.............	52:	717:	2,874:	— :	251:	
Western Germany 7/..:6/	60:	6,066:	11,316:	— :	11,589:	
Greece.............	— :	— :	— :	— :	— :	12
Iceland............	— :	— :	— :	12:	51:	
Italy..............	5/ :	30:	29:	2:	212:	
Netherlands........	2,006:	4,603:	8,124:	— :	9,819:	
Norway.............	113:	615:	824:	17:	— :	
Spain..............	— :	— :	— :	— :	— :	34
Sweden.............	604:	520:	5/ :	106:	— :	
Switzerland........	— :	112:	313:	50:	2,920:	
United Kingdom......	59:	1,210:	2,339:	1:	450:	
Total..........	3,533:	15,605:	31,313:	253:	25,743:	49
Asia:	:	:	:	:	:	
Japan..............	— :	16,350:	21,937:	8/ :	50:	
Taiwan.............	— :	2,333:	3,874:	— :	— :	
Other..............	5/ :	1,434:	2,254:	27:	28:	
Total..........	5/ :	20,117:	28,065:	27:	78:	
Africa.............	1:	— :	122:	322:	3,310:	
Australia and Oceania..	5/ :	5/ :	— :	21:	122:	
Grand total....	4,793:	43,219:9/	67,289:	3,234:	38,661:10/6	

1/ Crude and refined converted to crude. 2/ Not separately classified prior t
1937. 3/ Preliminary. 4/ Revised. 5/ Less than 500 bushels. 6/ Austria inc
with Germany. 7/ Prior to January 1952 reported as Germany. 8/ Less than .5
9/ Includes 1,000 bushels the destination of which has not yet been designated
10/ Includes 127 tons the destination of which has not yet been designated.

Compiled from official records of the Department of Commerce.

inued from Page 253)

Table 1 - UNITED STATES: Flaxseed exports by
country of destination, 1951-1955

(Bushels)

	:	:	:	:	:	
;h and Central America:	:	:	:	:	:	
inada.....................:	858,808:	30,275:	11,769:	4,233:	74,9
)sta Rica.................:	547:	320:	977:	448:	-
iba.......................:	286:	80:	36:	- :	-
?xico.....................:	125:	639:	- :	- :	26,0
inama, Republic of........:	- :	36:	11:	- :	-
Total.................:	:				
;h America:	:				
)lombia...................:					
?nezuela..................:					
Total.................:					
)pe:	:	:	:	:	
?lgium-Luxembourg.........:	1,685,758:	844,388:	- :	2,503,753:	1,320,5
rance.....................:	- :	- :	- :	222,674:	877,9
celand....................:	24:	40:	- :	- :	-
taly......................:	- :	- :	- :	403,627:	3 4,0
reland....................:	32,632:	- :	- :	- :	-
etherlands................:	587,607:	462,935:	- :	3,775,309:	1,598,2
orway.....................:	419,343:	- :	- :	- :	406,0
witzerland................:	- :	20,504:	- :	287,780:	50,1
nited Kingdom.............:	36:	498,698:	- :	1,701,909:	24,4
ther.....................:	- :	- :	- :	99 119:	-
Total.................:	:				
a	:				
apan.....................:	:				
ther.....................:	:				
Total.................:	:				
ica......................:	:				
ania.....................:	:				
Grand total..........:					

Preliminary.   Revised

piled from official records of the Department of Commerce.

254

(Continued from preceding pa

UNITED STATES: Soybean and soybean oil exports by country
of destination, average 1935-39, annual 1954-1955

Country of destination	Soybeans			Soybean oil 1/		
	Average 1937-39 2/	1954 3/ 4/	1955 3/	Average 1935-39	1954 3/ 4/	1955
	1,000 bushels			Short tons		
North America:						
Canada............:	1,197:	7,497:	7,787:	76:	7,205:	11,
Cuba.............:	5/ :	5/ :	5/ :	1,917:	1,587:	3,
Other............:	62:	- :	1:	467:	313:	2,
Total..........:	1,259:	7,497:	7,788:	2,460:	9,105:	17,
South America........:	5/ :	- :	5/ :	151:	303:	1,
Europe:	:	:	:	:	:	:
Austria..........:	6/ :	- :	37:	- :	- :	-
Belgium-Luxembourg..:	15:	204:	1,324:	- :	451:	
Denmark..........:	606:	1,365:	3,947:	- :	- :	-
Finland..........:	18:	163:	186:	65:	- :	-
France...........:	52:	717:	2,874:	- :	251:	
Western Germany 7/..:6/	60:	6,066:	11,316:	- :	11,589:	-
Greece...........:	- :	- :	- :	- :	- :	12,
Iceland..........:	- :	- :	- :	12:	51:	
Italy............:	5/ :	30:	29:	2:	212:	-
Netherlands......:	2,006:	4,603:	8,124:	- :	9,819:	
Norway...........:	113:	615:	824:	17:	- :	-
Spain............:	- :	- :	- :	- :	- :	34,
Sweden...........:	604:	520:	5/ :	106:	- :	-
Switzerland......:	- :	112:	313:	50:	2,920:	
United Kingdom...:	59:	1,210:	2,339:	1:	450:	
Total..........:	3,533:	15,605:	31,313:	253:	25,743:	49,
Asia:	:	:	:	:	:	:
Japan............:	- :	16,350:	21,937:	8/ :	50:	
Taiwan...........:	- :	2,333:	3,874:	- :	- :	-
Other............:	5/ :	1,434:	2,254:	27:	28:	
Total..........:	5/ :	20,117:	28,065:	27:	78:	
Africa...............:	1:	- :	122:	322:	3,310:	
Australia and Oceania..:	5/ :	5/ :	- :	21:	122:	
Grand total....:	4,793:	43,219:9/	67,289:	3,234:	38,661:10/68	

1/ Crude and refined converted to crude. 2/ Not separately classified prior to
1937. 3/ Preliminary. 4/ Revised. 5/ Less than 500 bushels. 6/ Austria incl
with Germany. 7/ Prior to January 1952 reported as Germany. 8/ Less than .5 t
9/ Includes 1,000 bushels the destination of which has not yet been designated.
10/ Includes 127 tons the destination of which has not yet been designated.

Compiled from official records of the Department of Commerce.

ontinued from Page 253)

Table 1 - UNITED STATES: Flaxseed exports by
country of destination, 1951-1955

(Bushels)

North and Central America:					
Canada....................:	858,808:	30,275:	11,769:	4,233:	74,
Costa Rica................:	547:	320:	977:	448:	-
Cuba......................:	286:	80:	36:	- :	-
Mexico....................:	125:	639:	- :	- :	26,
Panama, Republic of.......:	- :	36:	11:	- :	-
Total..................:					
South America:					
Colombia..................:					
Venezuela.................:					
Total..................:					
Europe:					
Belgium-Luxembourg........:	1,685,758:	844,388:	- :	2,503,753:	1,320,
France....................:	- :	- :	- :	222,674:	877,
Iceland...................:	24:	40:	- :	- :	-
Italy.....................:	- :	- :	- :	403,627:	3 4,
Ireland...................:	32,632:	- :	- :	- :	-
Netherlands...............:	587,607:	462,935:	- :	3,775,309:	1,598,
Norway....................:	419,343:	- :	- :	- :	406,
Switzerland...............:	- :	20,504:	- :	287,780:	50,
United Kingdom............:	36:	498,698:	- :	1,701,909:	24,
Other.....................:	- :	- :	- :	99 119:	-
Total..................:					
Asia					
Japan.....................:					
Other.....................:					
Total..................:					
Africa....................:					
Oceania...................:					
Grand total...........:					

_ Preliminary.   Revised

Compiled from official records of the Department of Commerce.

Flaxseed exports in 1955 at 4,706,215 bushels were the highest in almost 50 years with the single exception of 1954. And linseed oil exports at 73,606 tons were, with the exception of 1954, the highest since the war years of 1943 and 1944. On a flaxseed equivalent basis, exports of seed and oil in 1955 totaled 12 million bushels compared with almost 32 million in 1954 and only 4.6 million in 1953.

Table 2 - UNITED STATES: Linseed oil exports by country
of destination, 1951-1955

(Short tons)

Country of destination	1951	1952	1953 1/	1954 1/2/	1955 1/
North and Central America:					
Canada.......................	518	1,191	47	44	108
Cuba.........................	995	988	799	842	703
El Salvador..................	10	7	2	8	-
Mexico.......................	114	43	34	344	231
Panama, Republic of.........	13	2	2	6	-
Other........................	128	80	41	42	11
Total...................	1,778	2,311	925	1,286	1,053
South America:					
Columbia.....................	94	97	76	75	144
Venezuela....................	54	81	190	346	131
Other........................	172	78	63	41	43
Total...................	320	256	329	462	318
Europe:					
Belgium-Luxembourg..........	510	-	-	-	-
France.......................	-	-	-	-	54
Western Germany.............	3,575	-	-	-	-
Greece.......................	5	13	1	-	-
Netherlands..................	11	6,590	34,437	208,247	41,507
Switzerland..................	537	26	2	410	2,583
United Kingdom..............	-	-	9,129	9,467	26,764
Other........................	154	23	572	339	7
Total...................	4,792	6,652	44,141	218,463	70,915
Asia.........................	881	177	273	549	1,228
Australia and Oceania........	169	24	11	3	1
Africa.......................	548	61	6	12	-
Grand total..............	8,488	9,481	45,685	220,775	3/73,606

1/ Preliminary. 2/ Revised. 3/ Includes 91 tons the destination of which has not yet been designated.

Compiled from official records of the Department of Commerce.

Europe continued to be the major market for United States flaxseed accounting for 92 percent of the total. The bulk of the shipments to Europe went to the Netherlands, Belgium-Luxembourg, France and Norway.

The major portion of the linseed oil--96 percent of the total--also went to Europe with 56 percent of the total destined for the Netherlands and 36 percent for the United Kingdom.

FOREIGN CROPS AND MARKETS

Published weekly to assist the foreign marketing of U. S. farm products by keeping the nation's agricultural interests informed of current crop and livestock developments abroad, foreign trends in production, prices, supplies and consumption of farm products, and other factors affecting world agricultural trade. Circulation is free to persons in the U. S. needing the information it contains.

Foreign Crops and Markets is distributed only upon a request basis. Should you find you have no need for this publication, please tear off the addressograph imprint with your name and address, pencil "drop" upon it, and send it to the Foreign Agricultural Service, Room 5918, U. S. Department of Agriculture, Washington 25, D. C.

COTTON: Share of United States and other supplying countries in
ecified import markets, portions of 1955-56 marketing year as shown

(Equivalent bales of 500 pounds gross)

Reporting period 1955-56	Supplying country	Quantity imported		...ying countries share of market	
		Previous year's period 1,000 bales	Current year's period 1,000 bales	Previous year's period Percent	Current year's period Percent
Aug.-Oct	United States	13	6	12	7
	Mexico	24	19	22	22
	Belgian Congo	20	18	18	21
	Total 1/	109	85		
Aug.-Nov.	United States	131	38	32	13
	French Colonies	84	80	21	28
	Syria	15	36	4	12
	Total 1/	409	290		
st... Aug.-Nov.	United States	118	34	30	9
	Mexico	58	106	15	27
	Nicaragua	21	39	5	10
	Total 1/	394	386		
Aug.-Sept.	United States	52	28	46	31
	Brazil	16	11	14	12
	Total 1/	114	89		
Aug.-Sept.	United States	11	2	25	5
	Mexico	10	11	23	28
	Total 1/	44	39		
Aug.-Nov.	United States	8	28	24	78
	Brazil	8	4	24	11
	Total 1/	34	2/ 36		
Aug.-Dec.	United States	34	9	34	10
	Mexico	20	26	20	29
	Total 1/	100	89		
dom.. Aug.-Nov.	United States	177	69	36	16
	Sudan	52	85	11	20
	Total 1/	493	434		
Aug.-Nov.	United States	95	48	96	39
	Mexico	2	62	2	50
	Total 1/	99	123		
Aug.-Dec.	United States	5	1	5	1
	Pakistan	26	13	28	16
	Br. E. Africa	13	21	14	26
	Total 1/	93	81		
August	United States	11	3/	35	-
	Br. E. Africa	10	26	32	60
	Egypt	8	10	26	23
	Total 1/	31	43		
Aug.-Oct.	United States	178	63	39	17
	Mexico	112	84	25	23
	Total 1/	456	370		

imports from sources not listed. 2/ Preliminary. 3/ Less than 500 bales.

Lightning Source UK Ltd.
Milton Keynes UK
UKHW020942011218
333087UK00010B/1606/P

9 780331 425420